CAREERS IN

COMPUTER HARDWARE ENGINEERING

SOME OF THE MOST PROMISING careers today can be found in the field of computer hardware engineering. With computers continuing to spread throughout everyone's personal life and across government and business enterprises around the world, the demand grows for hardware engineers to design the technology of the future. Hardware engineering is an occupation that will provide steady growth, job security and high-paying opportunities for years to come.

Computer hardware engineers research, design, develop, and test computer systems and components, including computer chips, Internet servers, network routers, video game consoles, mobile phones, and tablet computers. Computers are found in all types of devices, so hardware engineers work on everything from household appliances, to intelligent automotive systems, to wearable technology like Google Glasses and Samsung smart watches.

Engineers typically are employed at research laboratories, with most working for large high-tech manufacturers like Apple and Intel. More than 95 percent of computer hardware engineers are employed in large metropolitan areas.

Hardware engineers apply engineering concepts and techniques to build the technology of tomorrow. They create new devices, chips and interfaces for new hardware applications, and they enhance existing systems and components to make them faster, cheaper and more efficient. Some engineers are experts in certain types of equipment and components, while others focus on applying technology to solve the challenges of a particular business or industry. Hardware engineers are constantly striving to determine how they can best apply technology to help resolve issues and take advantage of new opportunities.

Engineers use computer software, modeling applications, and other tools to design new hardware. They begin by creating blueprints of the computer equipment that will be built or modified. They then test completed models of the new hardware, analyze the results, and make any needed modifications. They also must ensure that the new hardware will work correctly with other equipment, and with the software that will operate the hardware. They may be involved in overseeing the process of manufacturing the computer hardware.

1

Would you make a good computer hardware engineer? Technical training and at least a four-year college degree are required to land that first job. However, personal traits can be just as important for success. Do you like solving puzzles – particularly challenging ones that require a dogged determination to find the answer? Are you good with computers and math? Can you think problems through logically to arrive at the best solution? Do you communicate well, speaking and in writing? Are you a team player? If you have these qualities, you may be well positioned to pursue a career in computer hardware engineering.

If you have good analytical, interpersonal, and technical skills, you can enjoy a financially rewarding career. A combination of training, hard work and positive personal traits will help you achieve the personal and professional satisfaction that accompanies the role of a successful hardware engineer.

WHAT YOU CAN DO NOW

IF A CAREER AS A COMPUTER HARDWARE engineer sounds interesting, you can start making preparations now to enter the field. A good first step is taking math, science, and courses related to computers. The more you can learn about how computer systems work – particularly in a business setting – the better equipped you will be to succeed in this career.

Good PC skills are definitely critical. Engineers use a variety of computer-assisted design (CAD) applications to create chips, smart phones and video game consoles. They rely on databases, spreadsheets, and word processing software just as many other professionals do. Taking a keyboarding class and learning how to use productivity tools like Microsoft Office will prove as helpful in college as in the workplace. Courses may be available at your school, through local colleges, or through online tutorials.

It is never too early to start learning about how computers work. There is a wide variety of computer hardware, but most share some common functionality in terms of integrated circuitry. As you learn more, you will probably decide to focus on one platform, one industry, or a specific area of engineering. For now, gaining an overview of the various options will help you choose the environment that interests you the most.

To learn more about computer hardware engineering, read industry publications (many of which are available online). Visit the web sites of professional associations such as IEEE. If there is a local chapter in your city or on a nearby college campus, you may be able to visit a meeting and possibly obtain a student membership. Networking with local professionals who are employed as hardware engineers also helps you learn about scholarships, internships, and local job openings.

HISTORY OF THE CAREER

ALTHOUGH COMPUTER HARDWARE engineering did not evolve as a distinct profession until the late 20th century, the roots of the field date back hundreds of years. In fact, before the 1930s, the term "computer" referred not to machinery, but to a person who did mathematical calculations!

The earliest machine for calculations was the abacus, a device with rows of counting beads, that dates back to the 14th century. The slide rule, introduced in the 17th century, had moveable parts to calculate logarithms. In the 1800s, Blaise Pascal created a mechanical calculator, and Joseph Jacquard used punched cards to run a loom. Charles Babbage and Ada Byron teamed up in 1837 to create the "differential engine," a hand-cranked machine that contained many features found in modern computers. In 1890, Herman Hollerith came up with a punch card system for the massive data-crunching needed for the U.S. Census. (Hollerith also founded the company now known as IBM.)

The first computer powered by electricity was the Z1, built in 1936 by Konrad Zuse of Germany. The Z1 is often considered the first true computer because it could be reprogrammed to do various tasks. It was able to erase and rewrite information, while other equipment could only store data once, on paper, tubes, punch cards, or other mechanical means.

The Atanasoff Berry Computer in the early 1940s represented the next breakthrough in computer hardware. The 750-pound device used binary arithmetic and separated its memory from its calculation functions. The 1940s saw the first major military use of computers, when Allied forces employed the Colossus, a vacuum tube computer, to break German codes during World War II.

The first electronic, general purpose, large scale computer was ENIAC (Electronic Numerical Integrator and Calculator). ENIAC was built over a three-year period by University of Pennsylvania professors John Mauchly and J. Presper Eckert. Activated in 1946, ENIAC weighed 30 tons, filled a 50-by-30-foot room, and contained 19,000 vacuum tubes. The computer was used for artillery trajectory calculations, H-bomb design, and other scientific uses. However, there was no software to reprogram ENIAC: the programmers had to manually reset some of the 6,000 switches to change operations. Mauchly and Eckert later built the first commercial computer, UNIVAC, which was sold to governments and businesses beginning in 1951. IBM launched its computer business two years later and came to dominate the commercial large-scale mainframe computer market.

Through the 1950s, vacuum tubes, punch cards, and magnetic tape defined computer hardware. However, in the early 1960s, transistors began replacing vacuum tubes. Transistors cost less, weighed less, used less electricity and were more reliable than vacuum tubes.

The 1970s saw wider use of integrated circuits technology. Integrated circuits contained thousands of transistors on a circuit board, yielding peak processing speeds in a small area. Integrated circuits were used in 1976 to power the CRAY-1, the first electronic digital computer. Today's integrated circuits – more commonly called "chips" – contain more power than the early vacuum-tube computers that filled entire buildings.

Because of their size, speed, cost, and the need for highly-trained professional engineers, computers were primarily used by governments, large businesses and universities through the early 1970s. However, the introduction of the personal computer made the technology available to the general public. The first computers aimed at consumers were the Altair 8800 and the IBM 5100 in 1975. The following year, Steve Jobs and Steve Wozniak created the Apple, the first computer with a graphical user interface. (Other systems used text screens.) In 1985, Bill Gates and Microsoft introduced their own Windows graphical interface, which was adopted by IBM and sparked the era of low-cost personal computers. The ability to connect individual computers over a network soon followed, first with commercial applications and later with home networks. The first laptop was introduced in 1981, a 24-pounder that soon gave way to smaller, more portable and powerful machines.

While the Internet seems like a fairly recent innovation, it actually began in 1969 with Arpanet, a military research project to connect computers separated by vast physical distances. The system grew to link government facilities and universities for special projects. In 1990, Tim Berners-Lee invented the networked hypertext system we now know as the World Wide Web, which uses common protocols and computer servers to allow computers around the world to communicate. Networks also progressed from hard-wired connections between a few computers to today's wireless networks that allow people to stay in touch through various devices while at home, in cars, and anywhere they find a Wi-Fi connection.

The progress of computer hardware engineering has been a continual march towards smaller, faster, more efficient and more powerful machinery. That trend has continued into the 21st century as the personal computing market shifted away from PCs to other consumer devices, such as smartphones and tablet computers. The powerful chips and high-definition screens on modern mobile devices provide thousands of applications that let you play games, do your homework, and socialize with friends – all at your fingertips, whenever and wherever you like.

WHERE YOU WILL WORK

MOST COMPUTER HARDWARE ENGINEERS work for corporations, government agencies, and universities at research-oriented laboratories that build and test computer hardware. The largest concentration of hardware engineers is found in high-tech manufacturing companies that build various types of computers and hardware components. Some are employed by computer design firms, research and development companies, and computer modeling houses. Every sector of society relies on computers, so hardware engineers create systems and parts that are used by consumers, retailers, manufacturers, banks, oil companies, hospitals, airlines, architectural firms, scientific laboratories, nonprofit organizations, and the entertainment industry.

It is estimated that there are about 85,000 computer hardware engineering jobs. The industries that employ the highest number of hardware engineers are:

- Computer systems design and related services (20 percent)
- Semiconductor and other electronic component manufacturing (17 percent)
- Computer and peripheral equipment manufacturing (12 percent)
- Research and development in physical, engineering and life sciences (12 percent)
- Navigational, measuring, electromedical, and control instrument manufacturing (7 percent)

Other significant employers include software publishers, manufacturers of household appliances and other electronic consumer goods, information services companies, specialized design services providers, and federal government agencies.

Almost all computer hardware engineers work in metropolitan areas, with the largest concentration in the Silicon Valley region of northern California. They usually work in research laboratories where they build and test various types of computer components. These engineers typically work in clean, modern facilities with state-of-the-art equipment. They develop and use the most sophisticated applications, telecommunications, modeling and other types of equipment. Hardware engineers typically work on the cutting edge of modern technology, giving them the first look at the computers of tomorrow.

The best-known technology companies in the world employ hardware engineers, including Apple, Google, HP, IBM, Toshiba, Intel, Microsoft and Sony. While most hardware engineers have traditionally worked for large multinational corporations, a growing number are employed by smaller firms, as new software modeling applications are allowing more companies to design their own hardware. Most hardware engineers work full time, with about one-fourth of them working more than 40 hours a week.

Some engineers who work for consulting companies and multinational corporations travel extensively to meet with clients, or visit manufacturing facilities. These visits may require brief overnight trips, while other projects may demand that consultants spend months working at the client's locations.

Others are able to work at least part of the time from home. Telecommuting over the Internet or through high-speed connections to the main office – allow these remote workers to be just as productive as those who are physically in the office.

THE WORK YOU WILL DO

COMPUTER HARDWARE ENGINEERS research, design, develop, and test computer systems and components such as chips, circuit boards, processors, networks, routers, modems, optical disks, and jump drives. They also work with computer peripherals, such as the keyboard, mouse, printer, and VDT screen you use on your home PC. Computer hardware engineers develop everything from the central processing units on large-scale computers that run the space program, to tiny chips that power your smart phone. Some engineers also supervise the manufacture or installation of computers, digital equipment and related components.

Hardware engineers typically work for technology corporations at research laboratories in large metropolitan areas, building advanced digital devices for consumer and industrial applications. Computer hardware engineers also perform many of the same tasks when they are employed by universities, government agencies, systems design firms, not-for-profit organizations, consulting firms, and research and development companies. The goals at all these organizations are the same: making computer systems faster, more cost-efficient, more reliable, and more robust.

Most of these engineers focus on hardware – the physical components that make up a mobile tablet, for example – rather than the software programs that run applications on those devices. However, hardware engineers are sometimes involved in helping software developers create or test programs that run on their hardware. They may also create or modify firmware – the computer code embedded within a device like a phone that directly controls the basic operations of the hardware itself.

Other hardware engineers may work with non-computer products, such as household appliances, industrial robots, and medical devices. These products interact with computer systems, microprocessors, Internet connection devices, and similar components of computer systems to control or enhance their operations. The hardware engineer makes sure that the consumer device will interact correctly with the underlying computer components. For example, modern automobiles contain a number of computer systems and components to help monitor the car's performance. They may use cameras to warn when another vehicle is too close, adjust anti-lock brakes to prevent skidding, bring satellite radio signals through your speakers, or warn you when the car is overheating. In fact, Google has developed a "driverless car" that uses computers, cameras and Internet connections to automate the routine tasks of operating a motor vehicle.

The process of creating new computer hardware (or upgrading existing components and systems) includes many tasks for a hardware engineer. Depending upon the specific situation, their daily work may include:

- **Design new hardware using computer-aided design (CAD) software**

- **Create blueprints of new or modified equipment**

- **Build physical models for certain applications**

- **Select or recommend the materials that will be used to construct a particular device or component**

- **Test the completed models, either through computer simulations or in a physical laboratory**

- **Modify hardware designs to account for any issues found during testing**

- **Work with software engineers to determine what software will run the new hardware and make any required hardware changes to interact with the software**

- **Consider alternatives to reduce costs without sacrificing the quality needed to manufacture a reliable product**

- **Determine any security features needed for the component**

- **Work with other engineering staff and similar peers to evaluate existing computer equipment and determine any changes required so that current equipment will be compatible with the new hardware**

- **Collaborate with software developers to test and refine the hardware-software environment**

- **Write detailed specifications that document the technical aspects of new hardware, such as power supply requirements**

- Conduct beta tests of new hardware to see how end users interact with the equipment. The users may be another company that will use your hardware in building their cellphone if you are creating computer components; or it could be the actual telephone user if you are building the mobile device.

- Make modifications that may be needed after beta testing to prepare the equipment for the final production phase

- Test that the new hardware works correctly with other peripheral devices, such as printers or display screens

- Work with technical writers to create specifications, user guides, and other documentation needed to help outside vendors, developers and customers use the new equipment

- Provide training and training materials to peers within the company or technical staff at other companies who will use the new component in their products

- Oversee the process to manufacture the new hardware, including recommending equipment for high-tech manufacturing facilities that control dust, humidity, temperature and similar environmental factors that can affect sensitive technical components

- Provide technical support to other departments of the company

- Work with marketing, sales, promotions, and similar departments to inform potential customers about the new hardware

As these tasks indicate, computer hardware engineers work as an important integral part of a large professional team, developing and improving computer systems and components. While some of the research, writing, and testing work may be done alone, hardware engineers spend a good deal of time in meetings with peers and managers. They share their progress on various projects, present the results of research and tests, communicate next steps in the process, and tackle issues that might come up as the new hardware is being developed. Hardware engineers spend plenty of time consulting with others, providing or receiving information from other technical staff throughout the company or at vendor firms.

Being an effective hardware engineer also means staying on top of the latest trends and breakthroughs in computer technology. Engineers must also set aside a certain amount of time on a regular basis for continuing education so that they can keep pace with rapid advancements. They may attend classes at work, sign up for online seminars, attend presentations at professional society meetings, and read trade magazines, blogs and websites to stay abreast of new developments. Computer hardware continues to evolve more and more quickly, so engineers must ensure that their knowledge and skills remain on the cutting edge of technology.

The role of a computer hardware engineer is similar to that of an electrical or electronics engineer. The main difference is one of scope. Electrical engineers work with electrical, electronic and electromagnetic devices, often focusing on the process of generating and using electricity. Computer hardware engineers are more concerned with using electricity to process information. While the hardware engineer may perform some of the functions of an electronics engineer – such as designing and testing circuits – the hardware engineer is primarily focused on the specific components that make up a computer system.

Some computer hardware engineers specialize in certain areas. These include:

Computer Architect

Like the architect on a construction product, the computer architect looks at the big picture of how the individual components of a system fit together. It is the job of architects to make a computer system perform efficiently to meet the needs of the user. They help design systems that serve company goals for faster execution, lower costs, reliability, increased customer functionality, and similar criteria. They may design a supercomputer that does weather modeling for the federal government, or they may modify a video game console system to improve the graphics and game play of a particular model.

Chip Architect

A chip architect focuses on creating microprocessor chips. They determine what characteristics a chip should have. These architects then create a performance model to test the chip, divide the proposed chip into functional blocks, document those blocks so a micro architect can decide the best ways to program the chip, and create reference materials.

Micro Architect

A micro architect is an engineer whose role concerns the microarchitecture (or organization) of a computer chip.

Network Engineer

These hardware engineers install, maintain and support the computer server networks that run a particular business, school, government agency, or similar organization. They help select and build the hardware infrastructure (and sometimes software infrastructure) of a network. They also install the required equipment and monitor the network to ensure it operates efficiently. They may also help network users set up their passwords, manage email usage, store data, and protect PCs from viruses and spam.

Hardware Installation Manager

This manager leads a team of professionals who install and customize equipment at customer facilities.

Operations Manager

The operation manager heads the technical team that is responsible for the operations of a computer network.

Hardware Technical Marketing Engineer

This is a special type of employee who consults with clients and potential customers on the best solutions for their particular needs, and helps the marketing and sales organization tailor the company's offerings to those customers.

Computer hardware engineers at all levels may be called upon to direct the work of other technicians, software programmers, systems designers and similar staff working on a project. Leadership, time management, and communications skills are particularly important for those engineers as they bring together a diverse group of professionals working towards a common goal.

Over time, hardware engineers are often promoted to positions of higher responsibility. Some engineers decide to move up into permanent management positions, where they are responsible for teams of hardware engineers or departments filled with professional staff of various disciplines. Others may decide to go into business for themselves, providing hardware engineering consultant services to a variety of clients in one or more industries. Whether they move into management or continue with the daily work of hardware engineering, most computer hardware engineers enjoy a challenging and rewarding career creating the digital devices of the future.

I Am a Silicon Valley Hardware

Engineer "I've always been fascinated with how things work, so my family always joked that I would grow up to become an engineer. I never had any doubts myself – the only real question was what type of engineer! As I prepared to enter college, even that uncertainty had come into focus. Long hours on my laptop convinced me that I wanted to be a computer hardware engineer.

We live in northern California, not that far from San Jose, so I knew I wanted to work in Silicon Valley. I targeted colleges in the San Francisco Bay area, where I knew there would be close ties with the high-tech companies in San Mateo County. I was accepted into the engineering college at the University of California-Berkeley, and plunged into my studies with an electrical engineering and computer sciences concentration.

At UC-Berkeley, I learned all I could about computer components as I prepared for graduation – and for an internship or co-op opportunity in hardware engineering. There were a number of internships available with companies like Microsoft, Cisco, Apple and Google. All of these offered opportunities to work directly with the top professionals who design and manufacture some of the most exciting, cutting-edge computer systems in the world. I applied for several programs and was accepted by one company – the high-tech global manufacturer where I now work as a full-time hardware engineer.

I have only been here for two years, but I am already building a solid future in computer engineering. I started out in the department that designs microprocessors – the chips that power all types of consumer and industrial applications. The training program here paired me with an experienced senior engineer who added year's of real-world know-how to what I learned in college. A few months ago, I transferred to another department that integrates those chips with other types of devices in smart phones, tablet computers, and some of the newest mobile devices on the market.

What is really great in Silicon Valley (and at similar places around the country) are all the perks we get at the corporate campus. Competition is fierce among hi-tech companies for talent, so they go out of their way to keep us happy here. Our large, well-landscaped campus is typical for the industry – gourmet restaurants; fitness centers; hiking and biking trails; swimming pools; foosball, ping pong and billiard tables; massage therapists; on-site laundries; babysitting for those with youngsters – even a medical clinic.

We work long hours sometimes when we're under the gun to meet a project deadline. Like any job, not everything is perfect every day, but the pay is excellent. I'm having a great time here with lots of new friends. I'm also acquiring useful knowledge. Whether I spend my career here or move on to new opportunities with another employer, I am continually enhancing my skills so I can take advantage of what-ever the future has to offer next."

I Manage a Team of Telecom Hardware Engineers

"I started out working with computers many years ago as a hobby. In the early 1970s, my brother saw an article in Popular Mechanics about the Altair 8800, one of the first microcomputers. He ordered a kit to build his own Altair, but soon grew frustrated and handed it down to me. I had messed around with crystal radios and telescopes, but a computer was a new challenge. It only took me a couple of days to build my own Altair, and I realized I had a knack for computer hardware.

Back in those days, there were not many college courses in computers – and not that many jobs in the field. I was fortunate – I lived in rural North Carolina less than 100 miles from Research Triangle Park, one of the top research and development centers in the country. There were three universities near Research Triangle that had strong information technology programs. I was accepted at all three, and decided to attend the College of Engineering at the University of North Carolina at Chapel Hill.

While working on my bachelor's degree in electronic engineering, I was able to work with the university's internship program. I actually landed short stints with three different companies. I learned about how computers are used in the telecommunications, defense, pharma-ceutical, and financial sectors. Those internships gave me valuable connections and experience that helped me land a job after graduation with a national telecommunications company.

I worked for more than 20 years as a hardware engineer designing circuits that handle long-distance telephone calls. Over time, I was called on to lead project teams. I soon realized I had some natural talent as a manager. So I applied for an opening as an engineering team manager and was accepted into a formal leadership role. Since then, I have moved up the ranks and am now a senior department manager. While I no longer design and test the circuits myself, my years as a computer hardware engineer have provided me with the technical knowledge to better coach and manage my staff. Most of my time is spent helping team members identify and evaluate options, make creative choices, and work more effectively and efficiently. The best part of my job today is hiring new employees and training them to become valued contributors to our company.

In a few years, I will retire and hand over leadership to one of the younger managers whom I have helped groom. Whenever I think about my long career in computer hardware engineering, I always say a silent 'thank you' that my brother couldn't figure out his Altair 8800 kit!"

PERSONAL QUALIFICATIONS

THE COMPUTER HARDWARE ENGINEER career path requires both technical knowledge (also known as "hard skills") and favorable personal attributes (or "soft skills"). The basic technical skills you will need can be learned in high school, in college, and on the job. However, personal traits are just as important to building a promising career.

Hardware engineers need sound analytical skills. Engineers must analyze complex equipment to determine the best way to make it better or, if it is not working, how to correct it. You will need to be a critical thinker who relies on logic and deductive reasoning as you examine the assumptions of a project.

You need to be a problem solver who can identify complex issues, develop possible solutions, evaluate the strengths and weaknesses of different alternatives, and determine the best way to implement your solutions.

Creative skills will also come into play as you design new types of technical devices, or simply find more efficient ways to update existing equipment. If you like uncovering the most efficient way to get something done – or if you just like solving puzzles – your temperament will be well-suited for engineering.

Good reading and writing skills are also required. Computer hardware engineers must read technical documentation to understand the mechanics of how a piece of equipment works. They may have to document how they propose to build a certain type of computer chip or tablet screen. The ability to gather, absorb and share a vast amount of complex data will help you function better in many hardware engineering roles.

Computer engineers need to be comfortable working within a team and communicating with others – both in writing and speaking. Engineering may appear to be a largely technical field, but people skills are important too. You may gather information about current hardware by talking to more senior staff members, taking notes on your findings, and reporting the results to others. You must be a good listener, a solid communicator, and an active participant in group settings. Persistence will also be helpful because you may spend many hours digging into the details of a challenge or issue before you find the solution.

You need to be flexible and able to adapt to unexpected changes. You will need to manage your work and your time to get the most done. You will often need to juggle multiple projects with different deadlines. You may be called upon to manage other people in a virtual team setting. Along with being a strong team player yourself; sometimes you must lead a team working towards mutually-agreed solutions to complex problems.

Computer hardware engineers must be lifelong learners. Technology changes at a rapid pace, and engineers typically work on the cutting edge of new innovations. You will spend a good deal of your time learning about technological breakthroughs, new techniques and new materials.

ATTRACTIVE FEATURES

COMPUTER HARDWARE ENGINEERING provides some of the best paying and most prestigious opportunities available in the new millennium. The potential for creativity, personal growth and advancement seems unlimited as computers keep spreading through all phases of personal and professional life. Opportunities are wide open to work in a broad range of industries with large public corporations, private employers, government agencies and nonprofit institutions. You may design or update the systems or components that run personal computers, network systems, smart phones, tablet computers, video gaming systems, driverless automobiles, satellites, military applications, robots, medical devices, and any number of futuristic devices not yet imagined.

If you like staying on top of new technologies and challenging yourself to solve problems, you can enjoy a fascinating career in computer hardware. You may work on a variety of unique projects in a number of different areas. The pace of the work and the rewards are different from one undertaking to the next. You may work at some of the world's best known companies, interacting with experts in a number of technical fields as you help bring important projects from concept to reality. The work you do will have a positive impact on your organization, your community, the people who live there, and potentially consumers around the world. Your success can bring financial rewards as well as the satisfaction that accompanies a job well done.

The working conditions for computer hardware engineers are among the best in any profession. Major companies provide competitive salaries, attractive benefits, state-of-the-art equipment, in-house training, spacious offices, and other perks to lure the top candidates to their IT (information technology) companies. Most offer a career path towards advancement, offering greater responsibilities and rewards as a veteran engineer or as an executive. Silicon Valley giants and startups alike are famous for their generous amenities, such as high-tech campuses, gymnasiums, game rooms, and company picnics and retreats.

Hardware engineers are held in high esteem by their co-workers, peers and clients. They work closely with employees in other departments at all levels of the organization to implement new computer chips or upgrade a top-selling mobile phone. Fellow employees and managers value engineering professionals when a successful project delivers quality results that make their lives easier and help them meet company goals.

If you have an entrepreneurial personality, computer hardware engineering can also open doors for you to start your own business. Many IT professionals begin their working lives as employees of other companies before striking out on their own. After they build up a body of knowledge, experience, and contacts, they become independent contractors – either working for themselves or through a job placement service that pairs engineers with employers who need qualified professionals. Contractors enjoy the challenges that accompany working with a variety of people and projects. Best of all, they prefer being in charge of their own careers over the security of a conventional position with a permanent employer.

Whether you decide to climb the corporate ladder or follow an independent path, a career as a computer hardware engineer can be financially and personally rewarding throughout your working years.

UNATTRACTIVE FEATURES

WHILE A CAREER IN COMPUTER HARDWARE engineering can be rewarding, it is also likely to be demanding and stressful. Your customers may be internal (other employees at your company) or external (your employer's clients and customers). They will expect you to resolve their concerns over design and production issues quickly, efficiently, and accurately. Hardware engineers deal with complex systems featuring numerous interlaced components, so it may not be as easy to resolve those issues as it appears to an outsider. It may cost more money or take more time to solve problems than your customers expect – if it can be done at all! Those expectations can strain the normally sound working relationship engineers have with customers and co-workers.

At least one-fourth of computer hardware engineers regularly work long hours (including nights and weekends), particularly as project deadlines approach. Most engineers receive a set annual salary rather than an hourly wage, so there is seldom overtime pay. You may get "comp time" after the project ends, but it often amounts to fewer hours than the extra time you actually worked – and there is usually pressure to get the next project underway before the current one ends.

Computer hardware engineers face constant demands for education – both to get started in the field and to keep up to date with the latest developments in their industry. There is often too much to learn and too little time to keep up with new innovations. You also need to not only be proficient with hardware, but also understand the software that your company uses to program the hardware you design. Some employers offer training courses at the entry level, or when new products and techniques are introduced. Others may expect you to arrange your training on your own time and at your own expense. However, even when the company offers classes during working hours, you are responsible for keeping pace with your normal job duties, so you may have to work extra hours to ensure that routine daily work does not fall behind.

Computer engineering is complex, demanding and sometimes exhausting. Project life cycles can last months or even years. Lengthy projects can bring personal stress, conflicts with co-workers, and sometimes even burn-out. Hardware engineers seldom have the luxury of working on one project at a time, normally juggling multiple tasks and maintaining a hectic schedule. With employment forecast to continue growing only slowly, and increased foreign competition for engineering work, there will be fewer opportunities to find employment in some industries.

As with any career, you may have to deal with demanding managers, personality conflicts, unreasonable clients, government regulations, and office politics.

Engineers do work in clean, safe, modern offices. However, the long hours and constant stress can lead to unhealthy lifestyles. Frequent computer use can lead to eye strain, back pain, and repetitive motion injuries such as carpal tunnel syndrome.

EDUCATION AND TRAINING

A FOUR-YEAR COLLEGE DEGREE IS typically the minimum requirement to begin a career as a computer hardware engineer. Employers look for candidates with a combination of technical and business knowledge. Most hardware engineers begin with a bachelor's degree in computer engineering or electrical engineering (with a focus on computer hardware). Others have degrees in computer science, management information systems, or electronics engineering. Generally, a computer or electrical engineering degree provides the best opportunities for employment in a computer engineering position.

The first two years in a bachelor's program for computer hardware engineering are typically spent on the basics of engineering and computer operations, plus math, English and the arts. Junior and senior years normally focus entirely on computer engineering. The combination of hands-on experience along with classroom work provides the best preparation for the workplace. Look for classes in such areas as microsystems design, computer networking, circuit board engineering, embedded systems, robotics, and electromagnetics. Hardware and software engineers often work together, so some computer programming courses are also necessary.

For certain positions, employers may prefer candidates who hold a master's degree. A graduate degree in electrical engineering (or computer engineering, where available) will provide you with advanced skills and prepare you for more challenging job opportunities. Graduate students may concentrate their studies in such specialized areas as parallel computing systems, machine vision systems, or network systems. Courses often cover microprocessors, computer architecture, algorithms and systems organization. Master's programs typically combine heavy computer laboratory work with seminar presentations. Alternately, a master's degree in business administration (MBA) is valuable if you plan to move into management.

Those who plan to work in research and development, especially at a university, typically need a doctoral degree, such as Doctor of Engineering (DEng). Doctoral students focus on one area (such as networking) for their classroom work and the research required for their dissertation. Courses may cover internet technology, architecture, wireless networking and nanotechnology.

Most colleges and universities offer degrees in computer engineering. Students should look for colleges approved by the ABET (Accreditation Board for Engineering and Technology) to ensure the programs are up to industry standard. You will also need a bachelor's degree from an ABET-approved school to obtain professional certification.

According to a recent US News and World Reports survey, the top ten schools for four-year computer engineering degrees are:

Massachusetts Institute of Technology

Carnegie Mellon University

Stanford University

University of California at Berkeley

University of Illinois – Urbana-Champaign

Georgia Institute of Technology

University of Michigan-Ann Arbor

University of Texas-Austin

Cornell University

California Institute of Technology

US News and World Reports also ranks the top schools for graduate degrees in computer engineering. Those schools are:

Massachusetts Institute of Technology

University of California at Berkeley

Carnegie Mellon University

University of Illinois – Urbana-Champaign

Georgia Institute of Technology

University of Michigan-Ann Arbor

University of Texas-Austin

Princeton University

Purdue University-West Lafayette

Internships and co-op programs also provide great training opportunities for college students while helping them towards landing that first job. For example, Cisco Systems, the computer networking company, has 10- to 12-week hardware internships and four- to six-month co-op opportunities. These programs serve as the company's "primary pipeline for filling full-time positions." Microsoft's hardware engineer internships cover electrical, mechanical, optical and other opportunities.

While engineering certification is not required to work as a computer hardware engineer, it does demonstrate an additional level of professionalism. Graduates of a four-year college program can take the Fundamentals of Engineering exam through NCEES (National Council of Examiners for Engineering and Surveying). After four years of work experience, additional certification is available through the NCEES Principals and Practice of Engineering exam. Those who pass the exam become a fully licensed engineer. While most computer hardware engineers do not offer their services directly to the general public, the PE license is required for any engineer who does work for such clients.

Computer engineers can also receive certifications for certain types of hardware. ICCP (Institute for Certification of Computing Professionals) provides an initial designation of ACP (Associate Computing Professional). After four years, hardware engineers can also earn the CCP (Certified Computing Professional) designation. Other certifications are tied to specific operating systems (such as Windows NT, Linux, or UNIX), and databases (such as Microsoft and Oracle).

Regardless of whether you obtain certification, expect to take periodic continuing education to maintain your technical skills. Computer hardware changes constantly, so professionals are continually training to stay up to date on the newest equipment and techniques. Your employer may provide training, or you may need to find your own classes. Online training courses provide convenient, inexpensive options to keep your skills current.

EARNINGS

THE MEDIAN ANNUAL SALARY OF A computer hardware engineer is about $100,000 a year. That represents a slight increase over recent years. Earnings for computer hardware engineers are significantly higher than the annual earnings of engineers generally, which are about $85,000.

Starting salaries for entry level positions are typically lower than the industry average, with higher pay going to those with more experience and a graduate-level degree. However, even the lowest 10 percent of computer hardware engineers earn about $65,000, while those in the bottom 25 percent are paid almost $80,000. At the other end of the spectrum, hardware engineers in the 75th percentile earn over $125,000, while those in the top 10 percent of the pay range earn over $150,000.

Earnings for computer hardware engineers vary to some degree by geographic region, industry and local economic factors. For example, California reports that the average salary for computer hardware engineers in that state is almost $115,000.

Nationally, the industries with the top-paying jobs are software publishing ($115,000), household appliances and electrical and electronic wholesales ($112,500), specialized design services ($110,000), computer and peripheral equipment manufacturing ($110,000), and information services ($105,000).

When considering employment opportunities, keep in mind that your total compensation includes more than your starting salary. Performance bonuses often make up a part of the compensation package, particularly at large corporations in the computer industry. Other benefits include medical insurance, paid time off, pensions and retirement funds, and stock purchase plans.

OPPORTUNITIES

THE JOB OUTLOOK FOR COMPUTER hardware engineers continues to remain strong. Employment is expected to increase by almost 10 percent over the coming decade. By comparison, jobs for all types of engineers are expected to increase by about eight percent.

Many new engineers will be needed to meet the demand for new computer hardware, especially in newer platforms like notebooks and mobile devices. Foreign competition is expected to negatively impact the field. This will be offset somewhat by the increased development of computer chips that are embedded in other electronics, such as household appliances, medical devices, and automobiles.

Most of the new US jobs are expected at computer consulting firms as more manufacturers are contracting hardware design to outside companies. Increased reliance on consulting firms also allows hardware engineers and software developers to work more closely together on product design.

Job seekers with computer engineering degrees from colleges and universities accredited by the ABET will have better prospects for employment. Those with a graduate degree and experience will have the best job prospects.

There are currently about 85,000 people employed as computer hardware engineers. Only a few years ago, that number was 70,000. Computer systems design companies are the top employers of hardware engineers with almost 17,000 employees. They are followed by semiconductor and related electronic component manufacturers (14,000); computer and peripheral equipment manufacturers (10,000); scientific research and development services (9,000); and navigational, measuring, electromedical and control instruments manufacturers (6,000).

Most hardware engineers work in metropolitan areas. California employs the most hardware engineers at 22,000, or roughly a third of the US total. Texas ranks second at 9,000, followed by Maryland (4,500), Massachusetts (3,500) and Colorado (3,000). The top metropolitan area is the San Jose-Sunnyvale-Santa Clara area (which includes Silicon Valley) at almost 9,000 jobs. Other top areas include Washington DC (4,000), Dallas (3,750), San Diego (3,500), Anaheim (3,000), Austin (2,500), Phoenix (2,500), Boston (2,000), Baltimore (1,500) and Chicago (1,500).

There are also opportunities to work in smaller cities and towns. Some companies have offices in less populated areas, and many allow telecommuters to work from home at least part of the time. The non-metropolitan areas with the highest employment tend to be near major industry hubs such as Silicon Valley and the federal government in Washington DC. Those include St. Mary's County, Maryland; northeastern Virginia; north central West Virginia; and the northern mountains of California.

Once computer hardware engineers gain more experience, they may also find opportunities to go into business for themselves as consultants. Being a self-employed entrepreneur enables many hardware engineers to focus on the clients and projects that provide a good balance of financial reward and personal satisfaction.

GETTING STARTED

IF A CAREER AS A COMPUTER HARDWARE engineer sounds attractive, there is no better time to start preparing than today. The more information you can gather as soon as possible, the better decision you can make on your future career. Taking the proper steps now ensures you will be ready for the future.

Use the same methodology any computer professional would when beginning a project. Gather as much information as possible, organize and analyze your findings, document your options, and then make a decision.

Written information about computer careers is widely available. The libraries at your school and in your community have books, magazines, and other resources with information about computer hardware engineering. The business section of your local newspaper contains articles on general economic trends and the latest frontiers of technology. The Internet provides a broad range of easily accessible information from professional associations, government agencies, industry recruiters, private companies, and researchers. College catalogs and websites that focus on engineering careers can provide valuable data about courses and degrees, enabling you to select the right program to support your goals.

Talk to individuals who work in computer hardware engineering. Professionals who are employed in hardware design or with engineers, such as managers or recruiters, can supply current information about the state of the industry and its likely development trends in the future. You can find such individuals through local chapters of professional organizations, or by contacting high-tech manufacturing companies in your area. Some professional groups have outreach programs that target students, and they may allow you to attend their meetings at a student rate. Discuss your plans with your school counselor for insight into the job market, potential internships, and educational opportunities in your area. Get input from family and friends on how well they believe this career may fit your personality and your strengths.

After you gather and organize your information, give serious thought to whether a career as a computer hardware engineer sounds right for you. Do you have the solid math and science skills necessary to get into an engineering school? Do you like working with computers? Are you detail-oriented? Do you like interacting with people to identify and solve their problems? How are your written and verbal communications skills? Are you analytical and creative? Do you mind working long hours? Most importantly, can you see yourself happy and successful in a career as a computer hardware engineer?

ASSOCIATIONS

- **American Society of Information Science**
  www.asis.org

- **Association for Computing Machinery:**
  www.acm.org

- **Association of Information Technology Professionals**
  www.aitp.org

- **Institute for Certification of Computing Professionals**
  www.iccp.org

- **National Council of Examiners for Engineering and Surveying**
  www.ncees.org

- **Project Management Institute**
  www.pmi.org

- **Society of Computer Professionals**
  www.comprof.org

- **Society for Information Management**
  www.simnet.org

- **The IEEE Society**
  www.computer.org

PERIODICALS

- **Certification Magazine**
  www.certmag.com

- **ComputerWorld**
  www.computerworld.com

- **Datamation**
  www.datamation.com

- **EE Times**
  www.eetimes.com

- **IBM Systems Magazine**
  www.ibmsystemsmag.com

- **IEEE Xplore**
  www.ieeexplore.ieee.org

- **Information Today**
  www.infotoday.com

- **Information Week**
  www.informationweek.com

- **InfoWorld**
  www.infoworld.com

- **PC Magazine**
  www.pcmag.com

- **PMI Today**
  www.pmi.org/Knowledge-
  Center

- **Wired**
  www.wired.com

WEBSITES

- **CareerBuilder**
  www.careerbuilder.com

- **Dice**
  www.dice.com

- **EDN**
  www.edn.com